WIZARDS & SPELLS

DUNGEONS & DRAGONS®

WIZARDS & SPELLS

A Young Adventurer's Guide

WRITTEN BY JIM ZUB

WITH STACY KING AND ANDREW WHEELER

TEN SPEED PRESS
California | New York

CONTENTS

MAGICAL ITEMS 77

INTRODUCTION

You are in a fantasy realm. That means there are fantastical creatures and even more fantastical abilities.

What kind of magic do you wield?

How will you use your powers?

This book is a way to answer those two very important questions. It's a guide to the extraordinary abilities that enhance the world of DUNGEONS & DRAGONS and the magic-centered classes available to adventurers. It gives you a wide range of options to choose from, along with spells and magical items to outfit your heroic persona.

Read this book from start to finish, or open it to any spot, get pulled in by the exciting illustrations, and start brainstorming from there. The more you read, the more character ideas will spring from your imagination.

Every character is unique. Even when two of them share the same magical vocation, the decisions they make will take them on an exclusive journey that is yours to tell. DUNGEONS & DRAGONS is all about building memorable characters, and the tales of your magical exploits are about to begin.

Let's explore!

BARD

CLERIC

DRUID

SORCERER

WARLOCK

WIZARD

CHARACTER CLASSES

Character class is a major defining element for a well-developed persona. You can think of it as your job, although it involves more than just work. A character's class shapes their education, skills, and abilities. It will also guide how characters interact with each other. Each class has stereotypes (good and bad) that affect whether your character is seen as trustworthy or deceptive, loyal or unreliable. In the case of magic users, who are the focus of this book, class can also affect the nature of their magic and the kinds of spells they are able to cast.

In addition, your character will belong to one of twelve races, ranging from humans, elves, or dwarves to tabaxi (cat folk), kenku (bird people), or half-orcs (see *Warriors & Weapons* for more details). Although some races are better suited to certain classes than others, your character can be any combination you want. It can be fun to spend some time dreaming up a creative history to explain how your character gained the training and skills needed for their chosen class!

BARD

DO YOU BELIEVE THERE IS MAGIC IN MUSIC?

DO YOU OFTEN FIND YOURSELF THE CENTER OF ATTENTION?

DO YOU LOVE TO PERFORM?

YOU MIGHT BE A **BARD**!

BARDIC COLLEGES

Bards may learn music and magic on the road, from a mentor, or with formal schooling. All bards belong to informal associations called *Colleges*, through which they share their stories and traditions. There are two Colleges.

COLLEGE OF LORE
These bards believe in the power of words to change the world. They are smart, sharp, witty, and adept at casting spells.

COLLEGE OF VALOR
These bards believe in the power of deeds to change the world. They seek to inspire others through their actions, and to keep the stories of great heroes alive.

Traveling from town to town, singing songs and telling tales, bardic life is traditionally associated with the adventures of other people spun into stories that a bard will tell or sing in exchange for a few coins. Yet there are many bards who pursue a life of adventure themselves. After all, what could be more glorious than singing songs where *you* are the star?

Bards understand that story and song have the power to reshape reality. There is magic in these gifts, and bards harness that magic to achieve great deeds. A talent for music is something all bards share, but playing an instrument and singing songs are not the only styles of performance available to them. You might prefer to be a poet, an actor, an acrobat, a dancer, or a clown.

Although most bards prefer to assist their allies from the sidelines, they are able to defend themselves with spells that enhance both weapons and armor. That said, their magic leans toward charms and illusions rather than destructive power. The end of a life is the end of a story, after all, and bards tend to believe that there is always a chance for redemption so long as a story continues to be told.

EQUIPMENT AND ATTRIBUTES

Armor Bards tend to travel light, using only leather or studded-leather armor.

Weapons They favor graceful defenses such as rapiers, swords, and hand crossbows, along with daggers, hand axes, and slings.

Musical Instruments Almost all bards play some sort of musical instrument, from a simple reed flute to an elegant harp, and their instruments can be used in spellcasting.

Music as Magic A bard's magical music can have many effects, including healing the sick, charming others, or freeing people from mind control.

Inspirational Gifts Bards use music and song to inspire others around them to perform great deeds. If a member of your party is struggling, a bard will often know exactly what they need to hear to turn their fortunes around!

FLORIZAN BLANK

PLAYING FLORIZAN BLANK Florizan hates bullies and tyrants, and loves beauty and art. He's warm, charming, and quick to adapt to new situations. He enjoys talking to people to get a sense of their stories and experiences. Having seen life from both the palace and the gutter, Florizan knows that truth and kindness are free to every person, no matter their possessions or wealth.

As the youngest son of a royal family in a small southern kingdom, Florizan Blank studied music, poetry, and dance from an early age. When he was 10 years old, his family was overthrown by traitors; Florizan was the only survivor. Smuggled out of the palace by his music teacher, he was given a new identity and raised in a traveling circus, where he learned bardic magic. He gained a reputation as a great actor, and it was in this role that fortune brought him back to the palace where he had lived as a child.

Florizan saw an opportunity. He wrote and performed a play that exposed the tyrant's crimes and incited a revolution. When offered the chance to retake his throne, Florizan refused, preferring life on the road.

DANDY DUELIST Florizan's stylish appearance and way with words have led many opponents to underestimate him as a fighter, yet his dance training has made him an excellent swordsman. His favorite move is to cast a dancing enchantment on his foe, so that a fight to the death becomes a flamboyant two-step—to the amazement and amusement of anyone watching—until Florizan delivers the finishing blow!

BLANK MASK

Florizan carries a simple pink carnival mask that was given to him by a grateful witch after he used his powers of persuasion to save her from execution. When Florizan wears the mask, he can magically alter his appearance for up to an hour. He uses this mask to impersonate other people or to create fictional individuals from his own imagination.

CLERIC

DIVINE DOMAINS Each cleric is devoted to one specific god and each god is devoted to one particular idea or principle. The magic on which clerics draw is tied to these divine domains. Most divine magic falls into one of six domains.

LIFE
Gods that care most for the preservation of life. These clerics are expert healers.

LIGHT
Gods of beauty, rebirth, and the sun. These clerics use cleansing fire and blinding light.

NATURE
Gods of the harvest and the forest. These clerics access nature magic, and can control animals and plants.

TEMPEST
Gods of storms and weather. These clerics can summon lightning or command powerful winds.

TRICKERY
Gods of mischief and subversion. These clerics may alter their appearance or slip between shadows.

WAR
Gods of chivalry and battle. These clerics use magic to strike their enemies hard and fast!

Gods are a very real presence in the worlds of DUNGEONS & DRAGONS, and they can bestow blessings and power upon their most faithful followers. Among these faithful are the clerics who act as earthly servants of their chosen deity, and who are able to channel divine magic to heal the injured, protect the weak, and smite the wicked.

A cleric's magic is defined by the nature of the god they serve. They wear their gods' symbols, fight in their gods' name, and live every day according to the principles of their faith. This doesn't necessarily mean that they're reserved or quiet characters. Some gods are very raucous and wild!

Clerics will often follow their god's call to set off on an adventure, perhaps to right a wrong, vanquish a foe, or bring home a lost relic. Wherever they go, clerics take their god and their faith with them.

EQUIPMENT AND ATTRIBUTES

Armor Clerics are the chosen warriors of their gods, and often don heavy armor.

Weapons They carry formidable instruments of war, such as swords, hammers, or crossbows.

Holy Symbols Each god has a symbol that is sacred to its faith, and clerics will not only wear these symbols on their armor but also carry physical representations of them, such as a talisman or an engraved shield.

Channeling Divinity Clerics draw on the powers of their gods to cast their magic. The effects vary according to the type of god they serve, and can include powers of healing, destruction, deception, and light.

Destroying the Undead Clerics are the scourge of undead creatures, whose existence is an insult to all the gods. Clerics can channel their divine powers through their holy symbols to drive the undead away or to destroy them.

BEL VALA

PLAYING BEL VALA Bel Vala is a devout follower of Corellon, the patron god of elves and the protector of life, and she takes her faith very seriously. She believes that Corellon is the source of her strength and her survival. She also considers life to be a holy gift that one must never be quick to take away, even in combat.

HEALING OVER HARM Bel Vala is not enthusiastic about martial combat. She prefers to play the role of healer, focusing her time and energy to ensure her friends and allies prosper. The exception is when she faces the undead. In those instances, Bel Vala is a remorseless warrior who channels a divine light that can eradicate their evil.

Bel Vala was a young novice healer in Tower Crystalis when the earthquake came. Inexperienced and unsure of her strength, Bel found herself trapped among the sick and dying after the tower collapsed. Next came the flood waters, bringing with them an ancient evil. Suddenly, the dead were walking again. The broken tower was filled with abominations seeking to feed on the few remaining survivors.

Bel Vala prayed to her god, Corellon, for guidance. Inspired, she channeled a cleansing light through her body into the fallen shards of the crystal tower, where it refracted a thousand times. The undead were destroyed by this incredible burst of divine power.

Bel Vala woke years later from a deep sleep. She had lost her sight but gained a new clarity of purpose. She was Corellon's humble champion, protector of the living and bane to all undead.

DIVINE VISION Though completely blind, Bel Vala has refined her divination skills to an extraordinary degree, allowing her to sense the thoughts and intentions of those around her. Bel Vala believes that Corellon will guide her through danger and lead her to where she needs to be.

THE CHALICE, THE BOOK, AND THE DAGGER

Bel Vala has been named the caretaker of a set of linked items, said to have belonged to Corellon, which she can summon from a fold of light.

The chalice is Taker, and anyone who drinks from it can be relieved of all mundane injuries and illnesses. The book is Keeper, which keeps a record of those afflictions. The dagger is Giver, and it can pass those afflictions on to anyone it touches. Bel Vala must balance the book by each new moon, or any afflictions recorded in the book will pass on to her.

DRUID

DO YOU FEEL A STRONG
CONNECTION TO NATURE?

DO YOU CARE PASSIONATELY
ABOUT THE ENVIRONMENT?

DO YOU LOVE ANIMALS SO
MUCH THAT YOU WISH YOU
COULD BE ONE?

YOU MIGHT BE A DRUID!

DRUID CIRCLES Many druids belong to one of two major traditions that define their practices and grant them special abilities.

CIRCLE OF LAND

Druids in this order are attuned to the power of the earth beneath their feet. They use this power to fuel magic and access spells unique to their home turf. For example, a druid from the grasslands may be an expert at passing undetected, while a druid living near the sea may have a talent for breathing underwater.

CIRCLE OF THE MOON

Druids in this order draw on the power of the moon to enhance their ability to transform into animals. They are especially skilled at using their wild-shape powers in combat, and they can transform into exceptionally ferocious beasts, ones beyond the abilities of other druids.

Druids are champions of the natural world. By attuning themselves to the elements, or by serving the gods who protect nature, they can unlock great mystical powers, including the ability to transform into beasts.

Druids care most about living in peace with nature and maintaining a balance between earth, air, fire, and water. They often defend wildernesses and sacred sites from unwanted intruders, fighting those who would try to control, abuse, or corrupt the natural world—especially undead abominations and unnatural monsters.

Druids are most likely to pursue a life of adventure when they feel the balance of nature is disturbed or that the harmony of their existence is under threat. They feel a sacred duty to the life force that runs through all things, and they will pursue that duty to the best of their ability.

EQUIPMENT AND ATTRIBUTES

Armor Druids use armor and shields made from natural materials such as wood and leather.

Weapons They prefer light, simple arms that have everyday uses in the wilderness, such as spears and slings for hunting or knives and sickles for harvesting. They also favor wooden weapons, or weapons with wooden handles.

Nature Magic Druidic spells harness the power of the natural world, such as exerting control over the weather and the elements, summoning and speaking to animals, and controlling the surrounding environment.

Wild Shape Druids can transform into animals and take on that animal's abilities. This can include land animals such as tigers and bulls, swimming creatures such as dolphins and sharks, and flying creatures such as eagles and bats, or even a swarm of bees! Most druids can't use their other skills, such as spellcasting, while in animal form.

LEGENDARY DRUID

DAWAN PAX

PLAYING DAWAN PAX Dawan Pax is both a devoted ally of nature and a powerful half-orc fighter. These aspects of his character manifest in the fierce and sometimes brutal way he defends and avenges his animal friends He prefers the company of animals; and he does not eat meat, which is unusual for a half-orc.

WIND THROUGH THE GRASS Despite his considerable size, Dawan Pax can move silently and stealthily through wild terrain, at times even becoming magically invisible. He retains the grace and athleticism of the beasts into which he transforms.

Many strange stories have been told about Dawan Pax, a half-orc also known as The Hunter's Curse for his sabotage of sporting hunts. Some say he was raised by beasts, and that's why he protects them. Others say he's a simple-minded brute who knows no other life. Still others believe that he doesn't exist at all, and he's merely a superstition created to scare strangers away from the wilds. None of these stories are true, and many of them were designed to belittle the fearsome druid—because few hunters have ever found any other way to defeat him.

The truth is, Pax lived an unremarkable life in a small orcish village, where he was raised to be a hunter. His closest friend was an old gray wolf who lived near the village in peace and harmony with the people.

One day, outsiders slaughtered the wolf. Pax found the body. In that moment, he devoted himself to search out the hunters and end their sport. In the pursuit of this end, he has traveled to many lands, becoming a great warrior and honing his druidic arts.

HONORING THE BEASTS Dawan Pax often uses his wild shape to live among the animals he protects. He has also been known to pursue hunters in the forms of animals they have killed. To this day, he still sometimes takes the shape of the old gray wolf.

THE SOUL OF THE EARTH

Dawan Pax carries an ancient piece of polished volcanic stone called the Soul of the Earth, which allows him to cast a particularly advanced form of *scrying* spell. If Pax recovers an arrow or other projectile from an injured creature, he can use the Soul of the Earth to summon a vision of the person who attacked the animal. He retains this vision even when in animal form, allowing him to track down his new enemy.

SORCERER

DO STRANGE THINGS HAPPEN WHEN YOU'RE AROUND?

DO YOU COPE POSITIVELY WITH UNCERTAINTY AND CHAOS?

DO YOU TRUST YOUR INTUITION?

YOU MIGHT BE A SORCERER!

DRACONIC BLOODLINES

Draconic-bloodline magic comes from the intersection of a dragon's magic with either you or your ancestors. As you learn to channel this magic, the imprint of the dragon will begin to manifest. At first, you will be able to speak draconic, the ancient language of dragons. As your power grows, dragonlike scales will appear on your skin, increasing your resistance to damage. Powerful draconic-bloodline sorcerers have even been known to sprout dragon wings that allow them to fly!

Your draconic ancestor can be one of any of the different types of dragons, and your magic will be influenced by the dragon you select. See *Monsters & Creatures* for more details about dragon types and their powers.

Sorcerers are born with an innate magic, one they did not choose but cannot deny. This magic may come from a draconic bloodline, an otherworldly influence, or exposure to unknown cosmic forces. In some cases, the sorcerer may have no idea why or how their magic developed, leading them on a lifelong quest to uncover the source of their power. This wild magic (see page 74) can be unpredictable and dangerous, with startling side effects at the most awkward moments.

Most sorcerers find themselves drawn to a life of adventure sooner rather than later. The magic in their veins does not like to lie dormant. Those who don't learn to channel their power may find their gifts spilling out anyway, in unexpected and often unpleasant ways.

EQUIPMENT AND ATTRIBUTES

Armor Too much gear can interfere with a sorcerer's magic, so they wear no armor.

Weapons They can use only simple armaments such as daggers, darts, quarterstaffs, and light crossbows.

Font of Magic The deep wellspring of magic within each sorcerer allows them to cast magical spells at will. Fledgling sorcerers begin with the power to cast a few spells each day. As they gain more understanding of their inner magic, that number increases.

Metamagic Unlike spells learned by rote memorization, a sorcerer's magic is intuitive and flexible. With a little experience under their belts, they can learn to alter spells to suit their needs. Some examples of metamagic include shielding allies from a spell's effects, extending the range of damage done, or allowing the spell to be cast silently rather than spoken aloud.

DAMINI MAHAJAN

PLAYING DAMINI MAHAJAN

Like her draconic ancestor, Damini can be proud. She does not tolerate disrespect, especially from those who need her help. When approached politely, she is warm and welcoming, surprisingly down-to-earth for a sorcerer who literally spends all day with her head in the clouds. The air around her cackles faintly with energy and a pale blue light, reflecting the magic held within her diminutive frame.

LIGHTNING ELEMENTALS

Damini can summon lightning elementals to fight on her behalf or to assist with her occult research. These creatures, formed from actual lightning into a humanoid shape, remain for up to one hour after summoning and only obey Damini's commands. These dangerous elementals are attracted to metal and will damage any living flesh that they touch.

Born to a long line of draconic sorcerers descended from a powerful blue dragon, Damini Mahajan displays an extraordinary control over lightning. Her powers manifested at an early age, and she spent her childhood learning to transform tiny sparks into crackling bolts of electricity. Now in her seventies, her mastery over this volatile element has reached the level of legend.

Damini is best known for her leadership in the war against the Batiri, a tribe of goblin fighters lead by Queen M'bobo to invade the neighboring kingdom. In a desperate last stand, when the rest of her party had been knocked unconscious, Damini summoned a lightning storm so powerful that it killed more than eighty goblins with a single blast. The backlash from her spell left the distinctive spiral scar that still marks one side of her face.

Although her three children did not inherit her magic, the power has manifested in two of her grandchildren. Damini has dedicated her remaining days to training them as the next generation of Mahajan sorcerers.

MAHAJAN TOWER

Damini lives in Mahajan Tower near the peak of Mount Pentos, where she can be close to the clouds that fuel her research. Two of her grandchildren reside with her in the spiraling column, learning to control their own magical abilities. From time to time, Damini takes on students from outside her family line, teaching them to understand and master their newfound mystical talents.

WARLOCK

ARE YOU DRIVEN TO PURSUE KNOWLEDGE, WHATEVER THE COST?

ARE YOU ABLE TO BACK UP YOUR MAGIC WITH PHYSICAL FIGHTING SKILLS?

ARE YOU PREPARED TO SERVE SOMEONE ELSE'S WILL IN TRADE FOR POWER?

YOU MIGHT BE A **WARLOCK!**

PACT BOON Once warlocks have proven their loyalty, their patrons grant them a special ability known as a pact boon. This gift may take one of three forms.

PACT OF THE BLADE
The warlock learns to create a magical melee weapon out of thin air, so they are never unarmed.

PACT OF THE CHAIN
The warlock is taught a spell that allows them to summon a magical familiar, a spirit that looks like a small animal and obeys the warlock's commands.

PACT OF THE TOME
The warlock is gifted with a magical book, called a grimoire, that contains three spells the warlock can always cast, so long as the book is in their possession.

Warlocks are driven by the pursuit of knowledge above all other things. Their power comes not from innate talent or long study, but by making a lifelong pact of service to an otherworldly force. These patrons, as they are called, can take a variety of shapes, from ancient magical creatures to dark beings from forgotten places.

Whether good, evil, or simply indifferent to mortal affairs, all patrons require a price from those they aid. This may be as simple as a few tasks here and there, or as complex as running a vast following devoted to the patron. In trade for their service, the warlock is given access to arcane wisdom and magics beyond the realm of most mortals.

Some warlocks enjoy a good relationship with their patron, like that between a teacher and a favored student. Others struggle with the demands placed on them by their pact. In either case, their powerful spells and deep occult insight make warlocks a valuable addition to any party, even if their true loyalty may sometimes be uncertain.

EQUIPMENT AND ATTRIBUTES

Armor Warlocks don't shy away from getting their hands dirty, and can wear light leather armor to get the job done.

Weapons They wield a range of simple weapons, such as daggers, shortbows, crossbows, and hand axes.

Eldritch Invocations Fragments of occult lore uncovered during a warlock's studies, these powerful incantations allow the warlock to cast certain spells with ease.

Pact Magic A warlock starts their adventures knowing two cantrips (see page 34) and two regular spells, taught to them by their patron, and learn more as they gain experience.

ZANIZYRE CLOCKGUARD

PLAYING ZANIZYRE CLOCKGUARD Zanizyre is naturally curious and cheerful, but the weight of her patron's evil often weighs on her, inspiring fits of melancholy. She does her best to help others and always takes the opportunity to do a good deed. However, she is unable to refuse her patron's requests. Since Tiamat is a creature bent on destruction, this means Zanizyre sometimes finds herself committing terrible crimes. Even so, she will refuse any attempts to be freed from Tiamat's service.

Fearsome warlock Zanizyre Clockguard is among the few mortals gifted with the patronage of Tiamat, the legendary Queen of Evil Dragons. There are many rumors as to how Zanizyre gained Tiamat's attention, but the most persistent tale is that she rescued an injured dragon hatchling and brought it to one of Tiamat's temples. Zanizyre refuses to answer questions on the matter, saying only that it was fate.

Driven to explore the world in her endless quest for knowledge, Zanizyre rarely stays in one place for long. She is known for using her magical powers to help the oppressed and downtrodden, and many a small town is grateful for her well-timed help against an invading force. Some say she is making amends for the terrible service demanded by her patron, for Tiamat is an evil creature dedicated to wiping out all mortal life.

DOMINATE DRAGON
This powerful spell is a variation on the *dominate monster* spell (see page 66) and allows Zanizyre to force a dragon to do her bidding. Dragons are notoriously difficult to subdue with magic, between their resistant hides and own innate magical natures. Although Zanizyre rarely uses this spell, it always makes an impression. The sight of a three-foot-tall gnome charging into battle on the back of a mighty dragon is not easily forgotten!

TIAMAT'S FANG

Zanizyre's pact boon is a magical short sword known as Tiamat's Fang. This weapon can deliver damage related to each of Tiamat's five heads, allowing Zanizyre to choose between acid, lightning, poison, fire, or freezing effects each time she summons the weapon. This ability to tailor attacks to her opponent's weakness makes Zanizyre a deadly and unpredictable foe.

WIZARD

A WIZARD'S SPELLBOOK A good spellbook is crucial to any wizard. You can write new spells in your book, expanding your powers with each new entry. Spellbooks can range in appearance from plain, travel-worn volumes to ornate tomes decorated with precious gemstones. No matter how fancy, the true value of a spellbook lies in the magic words written upon its pages!

If your spellbook is ever destroyed, you can recover only the spells you have currently memorized. For this reason, many wizards create a backup copy of their book, stored in a safe place while they are off adventuring.

Wizards are the supreme magic users, steeped in occult knowledge and trained extensively in the art of spellcasting. Fire and lightning are within their grasp, along with deceptive illusions and powerful mind control. The mightiest can command powers beyond imagination, including visions of the future and gateways that connect to strange dimensions beyond our reality.

For wizards, improving their spellcraft is their driving motivation; all else is secondary. They learn from many sources, including experimentation, libraries, mentors, and even ancient creatures willing to trade insight for personal favors. Most wizards spend years in intense study before embarking on their adventures.

However, unlike warlocks, wizards refuse to be bound in service to any creature or ideal. Their greatest personal treasure is their spellbook, where they make note of all the rituals, magical words, and arcane knowledge that they uncover during their travels.

EQUIPMENT AND ATTRIBUTES

Armor To effectively cast spells, a wizard must be able to move freely. Most wear no armor.

Weapons They use only simple defenses such as darts, slings, daggers, quarterstaffs, and light crossbows.

Spellbook Wizards begin with just six spells written in their spellbook, and can memorize two for quick use during a battle. They can switch up which spells they have memorized, but only when they have a few hours to rest and prepare.

Spellcasting Wizards have limits in their spellcasting power, although this grows as they gain experience. To begin with, a wizard can cast only a few spells before needing rest.

LEGENDARY WIZARD
MORDENKAINEN

PLAYING MORDENKAINEN Brilliant and well-read, Mordenkainen does not tolerate fools. He prefers to listen rather than talk and is skilled at encouraging others to share their thoughts with him. When he does speak, his words evoke authority and confidence. He can be stubborn and difficult, and rarely changes his mind once he decides on a course of action.

A one-man peacekeeping force, Mordenkainen has created some of the most powerful spells known throughout the realms. His strong opposition to moral absolutes means that he can appear as a friend or foe, depending on his current goals and fickle mood. Above all, he is driven by a desire for balance, never letting the cosmic scales tip too far toward either good or evil.

Mordenkainen's origins are unknown, although he is thought to have been born along the Wild Coast of Greyhawk, an untamed land filled with hardship and danger. He came to prominence as the founder of the Citadel of Eight, a collective of magic users who sought to keep peace throughout the lands of Oerth. The Citadel disbanded after a hard-fought battle at the Temple of Elemental Evil, where one member lost his life. Two years later, Mordenkainen founded the Circle of Eight, which continues to operate under his guidance.

A skilled leader and political manipulator, Mordenkainen is always looking to expand his arcane understanding of good and evil as an agent of true neutrality.

MORDENKAINEN'S SPELLS

As one of the most powerful wizards to have ever lived, Mordenkainen is responsible for creating many new spells, including the following.

MORDENKAINEN'S MAGNIFICENT MANSION

This incantation creates an extradimensional dwelling that exists for up to twenty-four hours. The house appears with enough food to feed one hundred people and contains a staff of one hundred ghostly servants, although these specters cannot attack or leave the mansion.

MORDENKAINEN'S FAITHFUL HOUND

This spell summons a phantom watchdog that can see through illusions yet remains invisible to every creature but the spellcaster. The hound will remain for up to eight hours, although it will vanish if the spellcaster moves more than one hundred feet from the spot where the summoning occurred.

MORDENKAINEN'S SWORD

Casting this invocation conjures a shimmering elemental sword made of pure force, which hovers in the air before the spellcaster. The sword will deliver melee attacks against chosen targets on command. It lasts for one minute before dissolving.

CLASS FLOWCHART

IS YOUR MAGICAL POWER INNATE WITHIN YOU
OR DOES IT COME FROM TRAINING?

INNATE

Do you search for arcane secrets or
are you interested in nature?

SECRETS

NATURE

Is your magic personal or do you use it
for the benefit of a group?

PERSONAL

GROUP

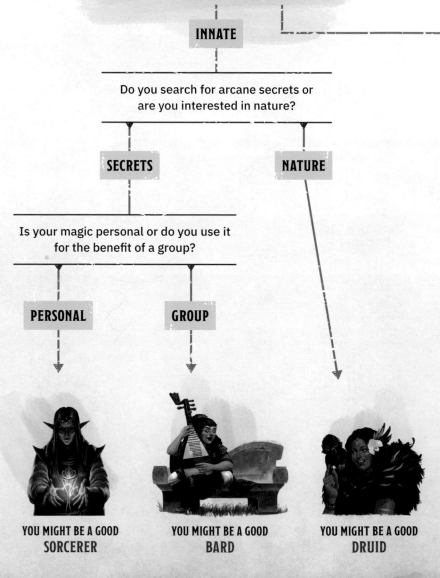

YOU MIGHT BE A GOOD
SORCERER

YOU MIGHT BE A GOOD
BARD

YOU MIGHT BE A GOOD
DRUID

Choosing a character class can be difficult, so here's a little chart you can use to help you decide.

TRAINING

Will you readily serve the demands of another?

NO   **YES**

Is your cause one of faith or do you follow some other power?

FAITH   **OTHER POWER**

YOU MIGHT BE A GOOD
WIZARD

YOU MIGHT BE A GOOD
CLERIC

YOU MIGHT BE A GOOD
WARLOCK

TYPES OF MAGIC

Academies of magic and eldritch researchers have grouped spells and their effects into eight categories called the *schools of magic*. A magic user can learn spells from multiple schools, although they may find that certain types suit their aptitude and personality better than others.

Abjuration: Block attacks or negate harmful effects.

Conjuration: Transport objects and creatures or bring them into existence from thin air.

Divination: Reveal information such as forgotten secrets, the location of hidden things, or glimpses of future events.

Enchantment: Influence or control others through entrancement or commands.

Evocation: Manipulate magical energy to create a desired effect, including the creation of fire, lightning, or beams of light.

Illusion: Deceive the senses with magical trickery, right in front of one's eyes or sometimes inside the mind.

Necromancy: Use the cosmic forces of life, death, and undeath to strengthen or drain energy from a target.

Transmutation: Alter the nature of things or creatures from their original form.

There's another important way magic can be categorized: Arcane or Divine.

Arcane magic, used by wizards, warlocks, sorcerers, and bards, draws directly upon magical energies to produce their effects. Divine magic, used by clerics, druids, paladins, and rangers, is mediated by divine powers—gods, the primal forces of nature, or a paladin's sacred oath. Both types of magic can be quite potent.

RITUALS AND SCROLLS

Most spells are cast in the moment and unleash an immediate magical effect, but there are other ways to cast or store magic—via rituals and scrolls.

A *ritual* is a longer and more involved magical-casting process. It can be used to create increased and sometimes even permanent effects, such as warding a room against intruders. Some rituals involve rare components, carefully chosen locations, or even specific times of the day or alignments of stars and planets in the sky above.

A *scroll* is a spell stored in written form, waiting to be unleashed. Once used, the scroll is destroyed and cannot be used again.

Any creature who can understand a written language can activate a scroll. An adventuring party without a spellcaster can use scrolls to help with healing, protection, or other enchantments needed for their quest.

SPELLCASTING

Of the many different types of magic found in the worlds of Dungeons & Dragons, the most common are *spells*. A spell is a distinct magical effect created by a caster that alters the normal world in some fashion. Spells can be quite subtle or literally world-shaking in their purpose and power. A well-timed spell can turn the tide of a losing battle or save an adventuring party from ruin. As your hero travels, their magical abilities will grow as they learn new spells by training with a mentor, discovering ancient writings, or exploring their inner power.

Beginning spellcasters can use only cantrips and first-level spells, and they gain access to more powerful levels of magic as they test their abilities and grow in experience. Some spells can be used with any type of magic, while others require a connection to either Arcane or Divine power to be cast. Magic is complex, and so are the rules of which classes can cast specific spells.

Though magic-wielding heroes can access only a handful of spells at any one time, hundreds are available to them; and many more are waiting to be discovered or even created. There's no way to cover every spell imaginable, so our focus is on four spells for each level that will most benefit spellcasters as their powers develop.

CONCENTRATION

In the following profiles, there are spells where "concentration" is indicated. These spell effects can last longer than the instant they're cast, but only while a spellcaster maintains absolute focus on the magic being used.

CANTRIPS

Cantrips take very little power and concentration, allowing them to be used at will, unlike higher-level spells, which require the caster to rest after using their allotment. In this way, a spellcaster always has a bit of magic to help themselves or their allies in a tough situation.

MESSAGE SCHOOL: TRANSMUTATION

When you cast a *message* spell, you can point your finger at a creature or person within one hundred twenty feet of you, and they'll hear a message from you and be able to respond briefly. No one else can hear the messages, so it's the perfect way to communicate a quick idea in secret.

SPELL TIPS

- You can cast this spell if you know the location of your recipient, even if they're on the other side of a barrier.

- This spell can be blocked by thick stone, metal, or wood if they don't contain any gaps. But a *message* spell can travel around corners or through tiny openings.

- The creature you target with this spell needs to understand your language in order to communicate with you. This spell doesn't translate words, it only sends a message in a language you already know.

LIGHT SCHOOL: EVOCATION

This basic spell makes an object glow with bright light for up to one hour. The target can be up to ten feet wide, creating a stationary light source. Alternatively, it can be something handheld that you carry with you. A *light* spell is a classic bit of spellcasting for good reason—it's always helpful to see where you're going in the dark!

SPELL TIPS

- The light can be any color you choose, so don't be afraid to get imaginative.

- Although the light this spell gives off is bright, it can be covered by a cloak or other obscuring material if necessary.

PRESTIDIGITATION SCHOOL: TRANSMUTATION

Novice spellcasters use this minor magical trick to practice their spellcasting abilities. With *prestidigitation*, you can create one of these situations.

- An instant, harmless, and obviously magical effect such as a shower of sparks, puff of wind, faint musical notes, or a strange smell.

- Light or snuff out a candle, torch, or small campfire.

- Make a small object clean or dirty.

- Chill, warm up, or add flavor to food (about one cubic foot's worth).

- Mark with a symbol or add color to an object for up to an hour.

- Create a trinket or a small magical illusion in your hand for a few seconds.

SPELL TIPS

- If you cast this spell three times, you can have up to three different *prestidigitation* effects going simultaneously.

- This spell is an easy way to show off to commoners and build your reputation as powerful and mysterious. An imaginative use of *prestidigitation* can amuse or frighten people or creatures who don't know the ways of magic.

SHOCKING GRASP
SCHOOL: EVOCATION

The *shocking grasp* spell conjures a bit of electricity to deliver a jolt to the next creature or person you touch. It may look like a practical joke but, if you're lucky, this shock can knock down small creatures in one hit. Use it wisely and its zap will be one your foes remember!

SPELL TIPS

- This spell only works if you can touch your target (unlike *call lightning* on page 47, which is a more powerful spell that can hit targets farther away).

- If your opponent is wearing metal armor, this shock can be even more powerful, so pick your target wisely to maximize its effect.

FIRST LEVEL

These spells for novice magic wielders will give your character a bigger taste of the power that magic can offer.

CURE WOUNDS SCHOOL: EVOCATION

With *cure wounds*, a target you touch is healed. Their wounds knit without scars or bruises left behind. More severe injuries may require multiple castings of the spell to heal fully.

SPELL TIPS

- A *cure wounds* spell can heal injuries received in battle, including burns or other traumas, but it cannot halt poison, cure disease, or return life to the dead. More powerful magic is needed for such tasks.

- Although this spell can be cast at first level, it can also be empowered at a higher level in order to mend more grievous injuries. The more power a caster uses, the more damage that can be healed.

DISGUISE SELF
SCHOOL: ILLUSION

Disguise self makes you look like someone else for one hour, fooling people into thinking your appearance has changed. This includes your clothes, armor, and possessions. They're not real physical changes though, so if someone tries to grab an illusionary hat, they'll reach right through and touch your head instead! If you're careful about how you use it, this basic illusion can be very effective.

SPELL TIPS

- ➤ Your new appearance must be relatively close to your actual form. You can't make it look like you're a giant or turn from a tall person into a halfling with this spell.

- ➤ Stay out of reach, or people quickly realize that your physical form doesn't match what they see!

- ➤ This spell affects only your visual appearance. Your voice, scent, and other physical cues will still be your own.

- ➤ Intelligent creatures may be able to see through your disguise, so don't assume you'll be able to trick everyone with this.

MAGIC MISSILE SCHOOL: EVOCATION

A *magic missile* spell creates three glowing darts of magical force that you can send hurtling toward a target. These missiles don't cause a lot of damage individually, but if you get zapped by all three they can really hurt. This is a classic combat spell used by many wizards to defend against threats.

SPELL TIPS

☞ These aren't physical darts, so they effortlessly move through wind, rain, and even armor. All a wizard has to do is point toward their target, and *zap*!

☞ After about forty yards, these missiles fizzle, so make sure your target is within range before you cast the spell.

☞ Powerful wizards can create more than three missiles at a time. So if you see a wizard with four or more missiles floating nearby, watch out.

SPEAK WITH ANIMALS

SCHOOL: DIVINATION

The *speak with animals* spell allows you to understand and verbally communicate with beasts for up to ten minutes at a time. Striking up conversations with local wildlife is a good way to find out what's happening in the area.

SPELL TIPS

➤ Most animals aren't very smart compared to people. Don't expect complex conversations or detailed descriptions.

➤ Just because you can speak to an animal doesn't mean they'll be your friend. Some animals are angry, hungry, or just want to be left alone!

SECOND LEVEL

Second-level spells are sure to dazzle the untrained; but a skilled spellcaster probably won't be impressed.

BARKSKIN SCHOOL: TRANSMUTATION

Casting this spells gives yourself (or another willing creature) tough, barklike skin that protects you as if you're wearing armor made of wood. This bark protection can last up to an hour, as long as you maintain concentration.

SPELL TIPS

- Barskin doesn't have the weight or bulkiness of metal armor, so it's a good temporary option for rogues, rangers, or other adventurers trying to stay sneaky.

- Having rough barkskin can also help you hide in a forest.

- Since this skin protection is magical, it's not actual wood, so you don't have to worry about termites (any more than you would normally).

INVISIBILITY SCHOOL: ILLUSION

A creature you touch (either yourself or someone else) becomes invisible for up to an hour, as long as you maintain concentration. Anything the target is wearing or carrying is also invisible as long as the *invisibility* spell lasts.

SPELL TIPS

- Attacking a target or casting another spell while invisible will end the effect.

- More powerful spellcasters can turn multiple targets invisible at the same time.

- Invisibility is great for sneaking around, just remember that the spell only hides you from being seen. It doesn't make you silent or muffle your footsteps.

MIRROR IMAGE SCHOOL: ILLUSION

The *mirror image* spell creates three illusionary versions of the caster that mimic their movements, constantly shifting position so observers can't figure out which one is real. Enemies can try to attack these illusions and destroy them, reducing the duplicates until the original is the only one left, but doing so wastes precious time—and in combat, every second counts.

SPELL TIPS

- This spell lasts for exactly one minute, so make sure you cast it only at the most opportune time.

- Attacks that strike a large area may destroy multiple mirror doubles at the same time, dispelling the illusion.

- Creatures whose senses don't rely on sight, like those with extraordinary hearing or an advanced sense of smell, can tell the difference between mirror doubles and reality.

WEB
SCHOOL: CONJURATION

Casting a *web* spell creates a mass of sticky webbing in front of you, anchoring on any walls, trees, or other spaces to which it can attach. Creatures who try to move past the webs may be caught in them and get stuck. Very nimble or strong creatures may be able to break free, but most regular humanoids will find themselves caught for up to an hour, or until the caster stops concentrating and lets the *web* spell dissipate.

SPELL TIPS

- Make sure you have surfaces to anchor your *web* spell. Otherwise, the webbing you create will just collapse on itself.

- These magical webs are flammable, so lighting them on fire can be a quick way to get rid of them. Doing so will also burn anything still caught in the strands.

- *Web* spells are normally used against enemies, but a quick-thinking spellcaster can also use them to save people who are falling or to detect invisible creatures.

THIRD LEVEL

More impressive in their effect, these spells also demand more power to cast and more time to master.

FLY SCHOOL: TRANSMUTATION

With the *fly* spell, you, or someone you touch, gains the ability to fly through the air. You can move about as fast as you would normally run, so birds and other naturally flying creatures can easily outrace you, but it's still a lot better than trudging along on the ground.

SPELL TIPS

- A *fly* spell lasts for only ten minutes, so make sure you're close to the ground when time is running out.

- Powerful magic users can cast this spell on multiple targets at once, allowing an entire group to fly at the same time.

CALL LIGHTNING
SCHOOL: CONJURATION

Casting a *call lightning* spell creates a storm cloud in the sky above. Every few seconds, you can choose a spot and lightning will rain down from the cloud to hit that area. If you maintain concentration, you can launch lightning this way toward different spots, striking enemies or sending them running for cover to try and avoid being blasted.

SPELL TIPS

- This spell only works outside or in areas with a ceiling one hundred feet or higher. Without that much space, there isn't enough atmosphere to conjure a storm cloud.

- If you cast this spell while there's already a storm raging, you'll take control of the existing storm clouds instead and can enhance their power.

- This spell can be quite powerful, but concentrating on controlling the cloud can leave you vulnerable to attack. Make sure you have other adventurers around to help protect you.

SPEAK WITH DEAD
SCHOOL: NECROMANCY

Casting a *speak with dead* spell allows you to converse with the spirit of a deceased creature or person and ask them up to five questions. Finding out how someone died and what to look out for can help you and your fellow heroes from meeting the same fate during a quest.

SPELL TIPS

➤ An apparition summoned with this spell can only speak languages and give information based on what it knew in life. Translation is not included as part of this spell.

➤ This spell doesn't work on undead creatures, since they're not actually dead!

➤ The dead aren't compelled to tell you the truth just because you ask them something. They can lie, tell riddles, or refuse to give information if they don't trust you.

WATER BREATHING
SCHOOL: TRANSMUTATION

This spell gives up to ten creatures (you and/or your allies) the ability to breathe underwater for up to twenty-four hours. Anyone affected by this spell also retains their normal breathing abilities as well, so if you normally breathe air, you can still do that while this spell is active.

SPELL TIPS

➤ Being able to breathe underwater is a powerful ability, but it doesn't automatically mean that you know how to swim or can do it well. If you're planning to adventure underwater, you'll want to get additional training in how to move and fight underwater.

➤ Breathing underwater doesn't let you communicate with fish or other aquatic creatures, but you could combine this with a *speak with animals* spell (see page 41) to travel underwater *and* chat with the locals at the same time.

FOURTH LEVEL

A spellcaster needs real experience under their belt to cast these spells.

FIRE SHIELD — SCHOOL: EVOCATION

Once a *fire shield* spell is cast, a barrier of fire appears around your body, lighting up the nearby area and protecting you at the same time. You can choose to activate this spell as a "warm shield" to protect against ice, snow, and cold climates or attacks, or as a "chill shield" to protect against fire and heat.

SPELL TIPS

- This spell can last up to ten minutes, which makes it useful for combat against fire- or ice-based enemies; however, it isn't going to keep you safe for a long time if you're outside in a snowstorm or exploring a volcano.

- You can use the light that this spell emits instead of carrying a torch, freeing up your hands for other things.

ICE STORM SCHOOL: EVOCATION

Casting an *ice storm* spell summons a torrent of rock-hard ice chunks that rain down from above, pounding the ground in a twenty-foot circular area of your choosing. Targets within the area are hit by these hailstones and their skin begins to freeze.

SPELL TIPS

➤ An *ice storm* spell not only hurts enemies, it also slows them down as they struggle to move against the wind and keep their footing on the slippery and uneven frozen ground created by its power.

➤ This spell can put out fires, just as long as you're not worried about damaging anything within the area of effect.

POLYMORPH
SCHOOL: TRANSMUTATION

The *polymorph* spell transforms a creature in your field of vision, along with all the gear and weapons they're carrying when the spell activates, into a non-magical beast. If you maintain concentration, this transformation will last up to an hour.

SPELL TIPS

- You can use this spell against enemies to turn them into something harmless or as a way to help friends escape by skittering or flying away.

- If a transformed target is knocked unconscious, they turn back to their original form.

- Transformed people can't speak, cast spells, or perform actions that require complex hand movements or speech, which means that casting *polymorph* on another spellcaster can be a powerful way to stop them from casting spells on you or your friends.

STONE SHAPE
SCHOOL: TRANSMUTATION

After casting a *stone shape* spell, you can touch a small stone object or area of stone five feet across or deep and form it into any shape you choose. That means you can make a small passage, mold stone to make a small statue, or even make a small weapon out of rock.

SPELL TIPS

- Get creative! You could pull up a section of stone from the floor to block a door while trying to escape from creatures chasing you, hide an item in a space you carve out in a wall, or drill a small peephole into a barrier to see what's on the other side.

- If you use *stone shape* to make a hole, remember that you'll need to cast the spell again if you want to close it afterward.

FIFTH LEVEL

Mastery of these powerful spells reflects hard work, study, and a deep internal store of magical power.

ANIMATE OBJECTS
SCHOOL: TRANSMUTATION

After casting an *animate objects* spell, you can choose up to ten small objects (or smaller numbers of larger objects) to come to life and follow your command. Doors will open or slam shut, chains will try to ensnare creatures, and free-floating objects will guard, attack, or defend as you direct them, for up to a minute as long as you maintain concentration.

SPELL TIPS

- Animated objects don't have any personality. They can't speak and won't be able to relay any information.

- If an enemy smashes an object, it reverts to its original form and is no longer animated.

FLAME STRIKE SCHOOL: EVOCATION

The *flame strike* spell summons a vertical column of fire that drops down from above, burning anything within a ten-foot radius of where you direct it. This spell is particularly effective against undead creatures, as it hurts them with both holy light and fire at the same time.

SPELL TIPS

- ☞ Area-of-effect spells such as *flame strike* can hurt multiple enemies at the same time if you plan carefully. Look for areas where enemies are gathered close together and use it there for maximum effect.

- ☞ Flashy spells such as this one can be quite impressive on the battlefield, but they also call a lot of attention to themselves. That can make you a target for enemies who want to avoid being hit by future spells.

TREE STRIDE SCHOOL: CONJURATION

Casting a *tree stride* spell allows you to step into a tree and then instantly step out from another tree of the same type up to five hundred feet away. You can do this as many times as you want for up to a minute, shifting between trees at will. This power is used by forest creatures and fairy folk to spy on targets or to escape from attackers. Some druids and rangers have learned to do this as well.

SPELL TIPS

☞ Use this spell to sneak up on an enemy in a forest or to get to the top of an incredibly tall tree faster than you could climb it.

☞ As soon as you step into a tree with this spell, you sense where all the trees of the same type are within five hundred feet; so you can plan your movement and stay ahead of anyone trying to keep an eye on you.

HOLD MONSTER SCHOOL: ENCHANTMENT

When you cast a *hold monster* spell on a creature, it will magically paralyze them, keeping the beast from moving or attacking for up to a minute, as long as you maintain concentration.

SPELL TIPS

☞ Using this spell on a powerful foe is a good way to keep it from attacking while your allies defeat smaller and less-dangerous creatures, giving you a strategic advantage.

☞ Creatures with strong minds may be able to overpower your will and escape, so be careful against highly intelligent monsters.

SIXTH LEVEL

Spellcasters of this level have a well-earned reputation that proceeds them on their travels, and likely a few heroic ballads to celebrate their achievements.

CREATE UNDEAD
SCHOOL: NECROMANCY

The *create undead* spell can only be cast at night; when cast, it turns up to three humanoid corpses into undead creatures called *ghouls*! After being created, ghouls feed on humanoid flesh. They hunt in packs and tend to lurk near places where bodies can be found—graveyards, crypts, and battlefields. These ghouls will follow your commands for twenty-four hours.

SPELL TIPS

- If you want to maintain control of the ghouls for another twenty-four hours, you'll need to re-cast the spell.

- A ghoul's touch can paralyze their target, leaving you helpless for up to a minute. That's more than enough time for a ghoul pack to turn you into their latest feast, so watch out!

FLESH TO STONE
SCHOOL: TRANSMUTATION

Casting a *flesh to stone* spell at a target attempts to petrify their flesh, turning them into stone. Every few seconds, the creature may try to resist the effect. But if its will is weaker than yours, the target will harden and turn to stone. If you can maintain concentration for a full minute, then the stone transformation is permanent (until it is dispelled through more powerful magic).

SPELL TIPS

- Turning a creature to stone permanently can be quite difficult. But if a creature is even temporarily slowed down by this spell, it can lend a strategic advantage to an adventuring party in combat.

- If a petrified creature is damaged while in stone form, it will have that same damage when returned to its original form.

HEROES' FEAST
SCHOOL: CONJURATION

Casting a *heroes' feast* spell creates a huge banquet of food that up to a dozen creatures can enjoy at the same time. It will take more than an hour to get through this enchanted meal, but at the end of this repast everyone who has eaten will feel healthy and cured of sickness.

SPELL TIPS

➤ Spells such as *heroes' feast* may not seem as powerful as conjuring fire or speaking with the dead, but group morale is very important. A magical meal like this can lift spirits and ready an adventuring party for difficult times ahead.

➤ Magical food has benefits that last beyond the duration of the meal itself. For the next twenty-four hours, anyone who ate feels stronger and braver.

OTTO'S IRRESISTIBLE DANCE
SCHOOL: ENCHANTMENT

When you choose a target and cast *Otto's irresistible dance*, that creature begins a comic dance on the spot, shuffling and tapping its feet for up to a minute, if you maintain concentration. Not only does this look ridiculous, it can also create confusion among enemies as they wonder why their cohort won't stop dancing around when they should be fighting you and your allies!

SPELL TIPS

➤ Like *hold monster* (see page 57), *Otto's irresistible dance* can be a useful way to keep powerful enemies occupied while your allies deal with lesser threats.

➤ A creature that's dancing can still try to attack anyone who gets close to them, but it's much more difficult than normal.

SEVENTH LEVEL

Nearing the peak of magical power available to mortals, these spells are truly impressive.

PRISMATIC SPRAY — SCHOOL: EVOCATION

The *prismatic spray* spell conjures seven multicolored rays of light that flash from your hand, blasting enemies with powerful magic. Each ray is a different color and has a different power.

Red: Fire
Orange: Acid
Yellow: Lightning
Green: Poison
Blue: Ice
Indigo: Paralysis
Violet: Blindness

SPELL TIPS

➤ Not all creatures are vulnerable to the same kinds of magic, so do your research on monsters and creatures so you know which kind of prismatic spray to cast against them.

➤ This spell can't tell friend from foe, so make sure your allies aren't in range when you let it blast.

RESURRECTION
SCHOOL: NECROMANCY

There are many lesser healing spells, but the ultimate curative power is to bring a fallen ally back from death itself. As long as a soul is free and willing to return, and they did not die of old age, this spell restores a being to life and cures them of all damage that afflicted them before they passed. Even still, returning from the dead is quite exhausting and it can take several days for a person to return to full strength.

SPELL TIPS

- This powerful spell can resurrect beings who have been deceased for fewer than 100 years; but the longer a target has been dead, the more draining it is on the caster.

- Many spells have components, special ingredients required to fuel their magic. A *resurrection* spell requires a valuable diamond as its component, and casting the spell destroys the diamond instantly. Powerful magic can get quite expensive.

PLANE SHIFT SCHOOL: CONJURATION

Casting a *plane shift* spell allows you and up to eight other creatures who link hands to teleport to another dimensional plane. A physical component is necessary to complete this spell; in this case, a forked metal rod. There are many dimensions beyond our own and great treasures to be found in those worlds, but great danger as well. Such a trip is not to be taken lightly.

SPELL TIPS

➤ You can specify a destination in general terms with this spell, but not land with pinpoint accuracy.

➤ This spell can be cast on unwilling targets as well, banishing them from your current dimension.

PLANES OF EXISTENCE

There are a multitude of worlds, as well as myriad alternate dimensions of reality, called the planes of existence. Some are made of pure energy or raw elemental forces (earth, air, fire, and water), others are realms of pure thought or ideology, and others still may be home to deities or the demonic. Saving a city or a country can make an adventurer a hero, but questing in other worlds and saving entire dimensions can make a legend.

DIVINE WORD
SCHOOL: EVOCATION

This potent spell calls forth a tiny piece of the power that shaped creation. Any enemies you choose within thirty feet that can hear this sound are struck by its magical force, which may deafen, blind, or stun them. Weaker creatures may even be destroyed completely by its might.

SPELL TIPS

- In addition to damaging regular creatures, *divine word* may cause targets who are from a different plane of existence to be sent back to their home dimension.

- Area-of-effect spells such as *divine word* are an incredibly useful way to stop large groups of smaller creatures from overwhelming an adventuring party.

EIGHTH LEVEL

Few spellcasters reach this level of power, but those who do are nearly unstoppable.

CLONE SCHOOL: NECROMANCY

The curious *clone* spell grows an inert duplicate of a living creature to act as a safeguard against death. Once the process begins, it takes about four months for the clone to be fully grown. After that, if the *original* creature is killed, then their soul will transfer to the duplicate and they will live again. Pretty neat, huh?

SPELL TIPS

☛ The clone has all the memories, personality, and abilities of the original being from which it was copied, but none of their equipment, so make sure the clone has clothes and weapons once it wakes up.

☛ A clone can be created to reach maturity at a younger age than the original. Some spellcasters charge a fortune to rich patrons looking to extend their life using this powerful magic spell.

DOMINATE MONSTER SCHOOL: ENCHANTMENT

After casting a *dominate monster* spell on a creature, you attempt to exert your will upon it and take control of its mind and actions. If you succeed and can maintain concentration, then the monster is yours to command for up to an hour. The creature will follow your directions to the best of its ability.

SPELL TIPS

☛ If a creature is hurt while under this spell, it will be easier for its mind to fight back and break your control over it.

☛ Creatures without proper minds, including constructs, oozes, and some undead, are immune to charm spells such as this.

EARTHQUAKE SCHOOL: EVOCATION

The powerful *earthquake* spell creates a massive seismic disturbance. Any creatures in its area of effect may be knocked off their feet, thrown into the air, or fall into fissures that open up in the ground beneath them. If this spell is cast in an area where there are buildings or other structures, they are damaged as well and may collapse, causing even more destruction and danger for anyone within range.

SPELL TIPS

- Large-scale destructive spells such as *earthquake* are extremely potent but must be directed with caution, otherwise your allies may end up feeling the effects and be hurt by it as well.

- Casting this spell while inside a building is also extremely dangerous, as the structure may end up collapsing on top of you!

MAZE SCHOOL: CONJURATION

Casting a *maze* spell sends the target creature to a pocket dimension filled with a complex labyrinth. If you can maintain concentration, this labyrinthine banishment will last up to ten minutes, more than enough time to finish off other foes during a battle and prepare for your enemy's return.

SPELL TIPS

- If the target trapped in the maze can find their way to the exit, they'll return to the point from which they vanished.

- Minotaurs can automatically solve these magical mazes, so don't waste this powerful spell on them.

NINTH LEVEL

The most potent spells imaginable, these awesome powers defy the laws of the universe.

METEOR SWARM SCHOOL: EVOCATION

The mighty *meteor swarm* spell summons blazing orbs of burning stone that plummet to the ground with unmatched force, destroying almost anything unfortunate enough to be in their way. Every creature in a forty-foot radius is pummeled and burned by the heat of these meteors, and anything combustible an individual is wearing may burst into flame.

SPELL TIPS

- *Meteor swarm* is one of those "go for broke" spells that can cause massive destruction, but also change the course of a desperate battle.

- A poorly aimed spell with this kind of power can easily wipe out allies or ravage buildings and terrain, so choose your targets carefully.

TIME STOP SCHOOL: TRANSMUTATION

When the impressive *time stop* spell is cast, the flow of time is halted for everyone but the caster. For up to thirty seconds, you can move and use your equipment without anyone within one thousand feet even knowing that it's happening. When time resumes, those within that space will believe whatever changed did so instantaneously.

This spell ends if you interact with anything you're not personally carrying, including other creatures, or if you move beyond one thousand feet from where the spell was cast.

SPELL TIPS

➤ A *time stop* spell is the perfect way to make your escape when things have gone wrong. It's also a useful way to change your position in a battle or drink a much-needed healing potion.

➤ Unfortunately you can't stop the flow of time for anyone else, so using this spell with your allies is impossible.

SHAPECHANGE
SCHOOL: TRANSMUTATION

Casting a *shapechange* spell causes you to transform into a beast or magical creature. You can keep changing form into different creatures for up to an hour, as long as you maintain your concentration throughout. You will take on any of the physical attributes of the creature you have become, but keep your own mind and personality throughout any and all transformations. With this spell, you could temporarily become a dragon, a unicorn, a beholder, or any other creature you've encountered on your travels.

SPELL TIPS

➤ When the spell activates, decide if your clothing and equipment falls away, merges into your body, or is worn (only if it fits). Clothes and equipment won't change size or shape.

➤ You can only speak if your chosen form also has the ability to speak.

WEIRD
SCHOOL: ILLUSION

A *weird* spell creates a potent illusion that reaches into the minds of your enemies and creates a vision of nightmare creatures formed from their deepest fears. These imaginary monsters attack inside your opponents' minds, but your adversaries can't tell what's real and what isn't as they struggle to escape. All your targets within a three-hundred-foot radius will be hurt by these mental terrors until they either muster the willpower to resist or are destroyed.

SPELL TIPS

➤ Since this is a psychic attack happening within your target's imagination, you can't see what it is they're fighting.

➤ Although targets of this spell are not being physically attacked, if they die in their mind they will also die in the real world.

WILD MAGIC

Wild magic is born from the uncontrolled forces of chaos beneath the order of creation. In some cases, it comes from being exposed to a surge of raw magic from an ancient, arcane source. In others, the sorcerer may have been blessed by a fairy or marked by a demon. Still other instances seem to be as chaotic as wild magic itself, power surging through the sorcerer's body for no apparent reason. Only sorcerers are able to access this magical power, which defies all attempts to study and codify it.

As the name suggests, wild magic is often tricky to control. A sorcerer fueled by wild magic is capable of astonishing feats, but using this power can have unpredictable side effects. These effects are known as a *wild magic surge*. There's no way to know when a surge will strike, or what form it will take, although they often occur at the most awkward (or funny) moments.

BEND LUCK

One pleasant aspect of wild magic is the ability, as a sorcerer grows in power, to use that chaos to swing the fates in your favor. Experienced sorcerers can learn to "bend luck," which increases the chances that their spells will have the desired effect on their target. Of course, using this ability carries a risk of a wild magic surge, making things even more unpredictable.

WILD MAGIC SURGE

Here are some examples of wild magic surges; but since the effects are random, you can always invent your own to add to the list!

- You grow a long beard of feathers, which lasts until you sneeze. Then they all fly off your face at once!

- Three creatures within thirty feet of you are struck by a bolt of lightning out of the blue.

- You are transformed into a sheep for ten minutes.

- For one minute, you cannot speak. Pink bubbles float out of your mouth when you try.

- When you speak, it's incredibly loud, no matter what, for one minute.

- Your skin turns a vibrant shade of blue, which lasts until the curse is removed through other powerful magic.

- You are teleported sixty feet in a random direction.

- A unicorn appears within five feet of you, but disappears after five minutes.

- You accidentally cast a *fireball* spell on yourself.

- Your hair all falls out! It will regrow to its original length over the next twenty-four hours.

- You can't be hurt for one minute.

- Illusory flower petals and butterflies appear in the air around your head for ten minutes.

MAGICAL ITEMS

There's one source of magical power that almost anyone can tap into: magical items. These rare and treasured objects come in near limitless forms and have near limitless uses. They include weapons such as swords and staves, spellcasting aids such as wands and rings, items of clothing such as cloaks and armor, and, of course, magic potions. By using such items, you might find you can walk on air, summon thunder, heal an ally, or even raise the dead.

Magical items are not easy to come by. You may uncover a powerful gemstone hidden deep in a dangerous dungeon, seize a magical sword from a vanquished foe, or receive a useful potion as a reward for a good deed. Gaining magic items requires a combination of courage and luck. Some magical items are common enough that you could buy them from a shopkeeper or a traveling salesperson on a lucky day; but beware, there are many counterfeits out there!

ATTUNEMENT

Most magical items require attunement, a special bond created when you spend an hour or more holding the item and focusing on its use. That may mean meditating on a magic ring, practicing with an enchanted sword, or studying a book.

You can only attune a maximum of three magical items at one time. The magical items on the following pages require attunement unless stated otherwise.

WEAPONS

Weapons are common and popular types of magical items, because even when the magic part doesn't come in handy, the weapon part just might.

Magic swords are especially celebrated. Many great heroes of legend carried famous swords that could sing, light themselves on fire, or never miss a stroke. However, there are magical versions of every type of weapon you might imagine, from bows and arrows to war hammers or hand axes.

DAGGER OF VENOM By focusing on the Dagger of Venom, you can make it exude a thick black poison that coats the blade for up to a minute. Anyone cut by the dagger may succumb to its poison. It does not require attunement.

DANCING SWORD

When hurled into the air, the Dancing Sword can be directed to strike like a missile at whatever nearby enemy you choose. If luck is on your side, it might attack up to four different foes before flying back to your hand.

HAMMER OF THUNDERBOLTS

The Hammer of Thunderbolts gives you such great strength that you might survive going toe-to-toe with a giant! You can also use it to hurl thunderbolts at your enemies. However, the hammer's powers can only be accessed by someone wearing magical armor that gives them a giant's strength.

OATHBOW

The Oathbow is an elvish weapon that invites its owner to identify a "sworn enemy." Any arrow you fire will seek out that enemy, no matter the distance. However, the bow expects loyalty and, as long as your sworn enemy lives, you will find it difficult to use any other weapons.

WEAPON OF WARNING

A weapon of warning can take many forms, but all types magically alert you to nearby danger. The weapon will even stir you from sleep when an enemy approaches, saving you from sneak attacks and deadly ambushes.

THE SUNSWORD

The Sunsword was once a particularly fine longsword with a blade made of magically resilient crystal, created by nobleman Sergei von Zarovich. Sergei was murdered by his envious brother, Strahd, who attempted to have the sword destroyed, but the hilt survived.

Imbued with magical will and possessed of a desire to seek vengeance on Strahd, the sword hilt generated its own blade of pure sunlight—the perfect weapon for destroying Strahd, whose hate and dark magics transformed him into a vampire lord. The sunlight blade also makes this sword a great weapon to use against any other undead you encounter!

The Sunsword is a swift weapon that cuts and blasts undead enemies with its radiant light. It can also act as a source of light in the dark. The sword possesses its own mind and can convey emotions to its wielder. For example, it might transmit a sense of fear if it senses danger nearby.

SUN BLADES

The true Sunsword is believed to be lost somewhere deep in the dark recesses of Castle Ravenloft, but other swords with a sunlight blade are known to exist. These swords are known as sun blades. By channeling daylight through their blade, they are capable of delivering deadly strikes against vampires and other undead monstrosities.

STAFFS

A magical staff is generally five to six feet long, about as tall as a regular human, and can be made from a wide range of materials, including wood, metal, or even crystal. They can be polished smooth or twisted and gnarled. Some staffs can be used as a melee weapon in combat, doubling as a quarterstaff. Even a non-spellcaster can use these artifacts to channel mystical power. Each staff has ten charges, which is the number of times it can be used before running out of power, and regains one charge per day, usually at dawn.

Staff of the Adder

Staff of Charming

STAFF OF THE ADDER

When you speak a command word, the head of the Staff of the Adder comes to life, transforming into a poisonous snake that you can use to attack opponents. The effect lasts for one minute, so be quick.

STAFF OF CHARMING

With the Staff of Charming, you can cast a spell that will charm another person, making them friendly toward you and willing to obey your commands. It also allows you to understand any spoken language.

STAFF OF FROST

The wintery Staff of Frost grants you extra resistance to damage from cold and ice. You can also use it to cast a magical spell that will do freezing damage to your enemies.

STAFF OF WITHERING

When you use the Staff of Withering to hit a foe, you can choose to inflict special withering damage that's harder to heal, along with the normal physical impact of your melee strike.

Staff of Frost

Staff of Withering

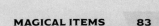

STAFF OF THE MAGI

The Staff of the Magi is a rare weapon that can be used as a standard quarterstaff in combat; however, its real value lies in its ability to cast and absorb magical attacks. When holding the staff, its possessor can use it to try and absorb any spell cast against them. If successful, the spell's energy is stored within the staff for future use, and the wielder is completely protected from the spell's effects.

The Staff of the Magi is capable of casting up to fifty spells, regaining one spell charge each dawn, along with any charges from spells that it absorbs. Magical attacks include casting fireballs, lightning bolts, ice storms, webs, and even a wall of fire. Its wielder can also use the staff to conjure an elemental servant, pass through solid walls, lift objects with psychic energy, detect magic, or cast an invisible shield to protect against evil.

In a desperate moment, the Staff of the Magi may be used for a single, explosive attack. By breaking the staff, all the magic stored within it is released at once. This retributive strike fills a thirty-foot sphere with explosive energy, wreaking untold amounts of damage and destruction. There is a chance that this explosion will cast the one breaking the staff into an alternate dimension.

WANDS

A magical wand is about fifteen inches long. They can be made from metal, bone, or wood and can be tipped with a charged piece of metal, crystal, stone, or some other material. Similar to staffs, each wand has seven charges that renew each day. If you run out of charges, the wand may be destroyed, so try not to drain it completely!

WAND OF LIGHTNING BOLTS

A twisted metal wand, the Wand of Lightning Bolts allows you to cast a lightning bolt (up to one hundred feet long and five feet wide) in any direction you choose. Be careful, though, because the lightning will set fire to anything flammable in its path!

WAND OF MAGIC DETECTION

Each use of the Wand of Magic Detection allows you to locate any magic power within thirty feet, causing enchanted items or locations to glow with a faint aura. The power lasts for up to ten minutes but this powerful wand has only three charges, so use it wisely.

WAND OF PARALYSIS

The Wand of Paralysis shoots a thin, blue ray that can hit a single target within a sixty-foot radius and paralyze them for up to one minute.

WAND OF POLYMORPH

The creepy-looking Wand of Polymorph can transform its target from one type of creature into a different, less-dangerous type. The target is limited by the restrictions of its new form. For example, a human turned into a sheep would no longer be able to talk or walk upright. The effect lasts for up to one hour.

One of the most powerful wands in all of existence, the Wand of Wonder can cast a staggering variety of magical spells. The effect is random and targets any one creature of the wielder's choice. Magical effects created by the wand can include:

Butterfly Swarm—a cloud of three hundred oversize butterflies forms around the target. The swarm makes it difficult for the victim to see or move through the space and lasts for ten minutes.

Darkness—a magical darkness surrounds the target in a fifteen-foot sphere. Not even darkvision or non-magical light sources can illuminate this gloom.

Gust of Wind—a strong wind pours out of the wand tip. All creatures in its path are pushed away, while torches and other flames are extinguished.

Heavy Rain—a sudden rainstorm falls around the target, obscuring vision and making everyone very, very wet.

Invisibility—instead of striking a target, this effect works on the wielder, making them invisible to all creatures for up to one minute. The effect vanishes if the wielder attacks anyone.

Slowness—causes the target to move at half their normal speed.

Stinking Cloud—a large sphere of yellow, noxious gas appears around the target, stinking of rotten eggs and skunk.

Thought Detection—the wielder can read the thoughts of their target for up to one minute.

USER BEWARE

Once in a while, the Wand of Wonder will not cast any outward spell. Instead, it simply stuns the wielder for ten seconds, leaving them convinced that something amazing has happened—even though it did nothing at all.

MAGIC ARMOR

Armor can be an adventurer's best friend, keeping you safe from a killing blow when faced with rampaging orcs, elvish arrows, or the slashing claws of a feral creature. Magic armor, though, is an upgrade; it doesn't just protect you from normal attacks, it can deflect magical blows and some have other special abilities you can call upon in the heat of battle.

If you need to wear armor anyway, you might as well try to get some made of magical dragonhide, right? And magic armor doesn't just include mail and chest plates. It can also include shields, bracers, or helmets.

ANIMATED SHIELD

An animated shield can float in the air in front of its wielder for up to a minute, protecting them from attacks. That makes it a great form of defense if you want to wield a weapon in each hand while staying protected.

BRACERS OF ARCHERY
Mastering a new weapon can take years of practice, and time is short. Thankfully there are types of magic armor that can take the hassle of training out of the equation. These bracers, fashioned from enchanted arrows, turn their attuned wearer into a master archer for as long as they're worn.

DWARVEN PLATE
Sometimes the best magical armor is also the toughest, and dwarves make *really* tough armor! A suit of dwarven plate mail magically protects you from damage and enhances your ability in combat, making you a more effective warrior on the field of battle.

HELM OF TELEPORTATION
Sometimes you find yourself so deep in trouble that your only real chance is a quick getaway, and that's when a helm of teleportation comes in handy. It can transport you and your nearby allies to a new location in the blink of an eye.

POTIONS

Potions are magical liquids made from enchanted herbs and other arcane ingredients, by experienced spellcasters who have spent years, if not decades, perfecting the art of capturing magic in a bottle.

A potion is a one-time-use magical item. You must drink the whole thing to get the special effect, so they can't be shared among multiple party members (unless you have multiple potions!). Once ingested, a potion takes effect right away, so be sure to save them for just the right moment.

POTION OF FLYING Drinking a potion of flying will allow you to fly for up to one hour. However, you can move only as fast as your character can walk on land. You can also hover in place. Be aware that you will start to fall the instant the potion wears off, so keep track of the time from ingestion.

POTION OF CLAIRVOYANCE

A potion of clairvoyance allows you to either see or hear what is happening in the moment at any location you have visited or seen before. You can also use it to see around corners or behind obstacles that are near your current location. The effect lasts for up to ten minutes, and you can switch between sight and hearing by focusing for six seconds.

POTION OF HEALING

An adventurer's best friend, a potion of healing will restore your body from damage sustained during a fight. Regular potions of healing repair minor wounds and bruises, while rarer types can do even more. Indeed, a potion of supreme healing will mend broken bones and fix deadly injuries in an instant.

POTION OF WATER BREATHING

The cloudy green potion of water breathing allows you to breathe underwater for sixty minutes. It smells—and tastes—as salty as the sea. Like the potion of flying, it wears off immediately once the hour is over, so don't let yourself get into deep waters without a plan of escape for when your time is up.

POISON POTION

Not all potions are friendly! Some nasty concoctions may look like a potion of healing but have effects that are the exact opposite. The unwary adventurer who imbibes this liquid will find themselves losing health fast. Only an *identify* spell, which can be learned by bards and wizards, is able to dispel the illusion that makes the poison potion look so sweet.

RINGS

Magical rings are a popular type of enchanted item, because they are small and discreet. As a result, your enemies don't always know you have them, or that you're about to use them, and you never need to be parted from them. (Nice jewelry can also really complete an outfit.)

A magic ring is like having a bonus spell at your fingertips—though it's really closer to your knuckle! Just remember that you can be attuned to only three magical items at once, so wearing a bunch of different rings doesn't necessarily mean you'll be able to access all their powers simultaneously.

RING OF THE RAM The Ring of the Ram generates a spectral battering ram that can smash through obstacles—including other people. Up to three times a day, you can use this ring like a long-distance super-punch to shatter doors or knock people off their feet.

RING OF ANIMAL INFLUENCE
If you want to charm an animal to be your friend, frighten an animal to chase it away, or communicate with an animal so that you understand each other, wearing this ring will empower you to do any or all of these things. This ring does not require attunement.

RING OF REGENERATION
An incredibly useful item for anyone who likes to dive into the thick of danger. The Ring of Regeneration allows its wearer to heal quickly from injury. Even if someone chops off part of your body, this ring will allow you to grow it back! (One important note: This kind of magical regeneration doesn't work if the part that's chopped off is your head.)

RING OF SHOOTING STARS
This ring has several powerful effects. For example, it can generate dazzling light, or create balls of lightning that can shock anyone who comes near. However, its most useful effect is that it allows its wearer to fire shooting stars from their hands, which can burn anyone they strike! This ring can only be attuned at night.

CLOAKS

More than just clothing items to keep you warm and dry, magical cloaks can bestow wondrous powers upon their wearer. They can be worn by all character classes with no magical training required. Like all wearable magic items, cloaks are designed to be adjustable for all sizes, from tiny gnomes to towering dragonborn. Some cloaks even have, woven right into their fabric, the magical ability to change their size.

CLOAK OF DISPLACEMENT

The Cloak of Displacement casts an illusion that makes you appear to be standing just a little bit away from your actual location, making it much harder for enemies to hit you. If you *are* hit, the cloak's power stops working for a few seconds. If you are restrained, unconscious, or otherwise unable to move, the displacement illusion also stops functioning.

CLOAK OF ARACHNIDA

The spider-patterned Cloak of Arachnida allows you to climb as easily as you can walk, moving across vertical surfaces and upside down along ceilings. It also makes you resistant to poison and prevents you from being caught in webs. Once per day, you can create a sticky web up to twenty feet wide that can ensnare creatures.

CLOAK OF ELVENKIND

The Cloak of Elvenkind is an elvish garment that lets the wearer, when the cloak's hood is placed over their head, draw upon the natural stealth and perception of the elven race. The cloak's power makes it harder for you to be seen when worn this way, while enhancing your ability to hide by shifting colors to provide camouflage.

CLOAK OF THE MANTA RAY

Worn with the hood up, the Cloak of the Manta Ray grants you the ability to breathe underwater and swim as fast as a medium-size fish. The effects stop when the hood is lowered.

WONDROUS ITEMS

Wondrous magic items are ones that don't fall into any of the previous categories. They can range from wearable items, like boots and gloves, to uncommon jewelry such as circlets and broaches. Bags, ropes, carpets, crystal balls, musical instruments, and other uncommon objects also fall into this classification. This magical designation is limited only by your imagination!

MASK OF THE BEAST

These ornately beautiful masks contain a spell that can render an animal docile and friendly; most useful when the wearer wants to survive an encounter with a predator such as a big cat or a beast such as a charging bull. It's equally effective on less-threatening creatures, from fish to birds or even monkeys.

The wearer cannot directly command animals nor speak their language, but finds it easy to interact in ways not otherwise possible. For example, they might convince a lion to let them ride on its back, or ask a bear to attack an intruder. More powerful druids and sorcerers can target multiple creatures, and run with a pack of wolves or swim among sharks without any fear.

BAG OF HOLDING

This bag appears to be relatively small, about two feet tall and four feet long, but it can hold up to sixty-four cubic feet worth of stuff. (That's about the size of four regular refrigerators.) Objects placed in the bag can weigh up to 500 pounds, but the bag itself will never weigh more than 15 pounds, similar to the weight of an average house cat. Overloading the bag causes its contents to vanish to another dimension, so keep track of how much you've stuffed inside.

BOOTS OF SPEED

Click together the heels of a pair of boots of speed and your walking velocity will instantly double. On top of that, your reaction to attacks is increased, making it harder for enemies to get the jump on you. The magic wears off after ten minutes, and will not recover until you've had a long, eight-hour rest. You can turn the boots' magic off by clicking your heels together a second time, saving part of the magical charge for later use.

LANTERN OF REVEALING

When lit, this lantern gives off a bright light that renders invisible creatures and objects visible. This light extends in a thirty-foot circle around the lantern. By lowering the lantern's hood, you can focus the light's range to five feet.

NOLZUR'S MARVELOUS PIGMENTS These very rare pigments allow you to create three-dimensional objects by painting them onto a flat surface. Each pot of paint can cover up to one thousand square feet, about the floor size of a small suburban house. When you complete the painting, the object or landscape becomes a real, physical object. Painting a door on a wall creates a real door you can walk through, for example. It is not possible to paint wealth or magic into being. Painted gold coins will turn out to be dull, worthless metal, and painted wands cannot be used for spells.

ORB OF DRAGONKIND The rare and wondrous orbs of dragonkind allow their user to *summon* a dragon. They don't grant any other control over the powerful beasts; all you're really doing is bringing one of the most formidable creatures in the world much *closer* to you. What they do when they arrive is up to them. Often, they'll want to punish the summoner! An orb grants other powers at random, such as healing or immunities; however, it also curses its wielder with unexpected weaknesses and disadvantages. Using an orb is very risky.

ROPE OF CLIMBING

By holding one end of this magical rope and speaking a command word, the rope animates, moving toward the destination of your choosing. You can tell the rope to fasten itself (securing to an object), untie itself, or knot itself in one-foot intervals for easier climbing. The rope is sixty feet long and can hold up to 3,000 pounds in weight.

STACKING MAGICAL ITEMS

Except in rare instances, a character can wear or use only one of each type of magical item at a time. Stacking multiple magic cloaks over your clothing, for instance, is not only very warm and bulky but can negate the effect of the magic.

For paired magical items, like boots or gloves, you must wear both the right and left items for the magic to work—so no sharing your boots of speed with a friend so you can both run double-time.

USING MAGIC
TO TELL YOUR OWN STORIES

Bel Vala could hear footsteps on the cold stone floor and smell touches of exotic fragrances used to mask the stench of death, but there was no breathing to match the animalistic movement she detected.

Undead.

The unliving were her most hated enemies and she would do anything to destroy their evil blight.

The cleric's hands clenched tightly. She could feel the familiar touch of Giver, her enchanted dagger, and Taker, the silver chalice. These linked items would not seem like much to a casual observer, but those who could see magic would be awestruck by their potent aura.

The vampire spawn began to move closer; one breaking the silence of the room with a hissing threat, her tongue pressed against sharp fangs.

"Lord Strahd has marked you for death."

Bel Vala smirked and her hands quivered for a moment as she felt the divine power of her god, Corellon, surging from within.

Pure sunlight exploded from Bel Vala's frail body and the vampires screamed in agony.

Reading about adventure is a great way to stir your imagination, and creating a character is an important first step in composing your personal stories. Building a new character is about discovering who they are at the beginning of their journey and then figuring out who they might become as their legend grows across the land.

Your idea might start with a single hero or a small group of adventurers, but it can go *anywhere*: a creature's lair, the village nearby, cities and dungeons, caverns or skyscapes. You get to choose all the ingredients and stir them together. To help you as you develop your story, here are some questions to keep in mind:

WHO ARE YOUR CHARACTERS?

- Are your heroes like you or different? Young or old, human or something else? Think about the foes you must face. Great heroes require great challenges. What makes your villains memorable and powerful, and what brings them into conflict with your adventurers?

WHERE DOES YOUR STORY TAKE PLACE?

- At the top of a mountain, in a serene forest, deep underwater, or in a creepy boneyard?

WHEN DOES THE STORY HAPPEN?

- At night or during the day, in the middle of a thunderstorm or right before the bells toll to ring in the new year? Think about time passing as your story unfolds.

HOW DO THINGS CHANGE AS THE STORY PROCEEDS?

- Do your heroes succeed or fail? Do they find somewhere new or explore someplace old?

WHAT SHOULD SOMEONE FEEL AS THEY EXPERIENCE YOUR STORY?

- Do you want them to laugh or get scared? Cheer or be grossed out?

WHY ARE YOUR HEROES GOING ON THIS ADVENTURE?

- Knowing what their goals are will help you create a compelling tale of courage and exploration.

Remember, you don't have to answer all these questions by yourself! DUNGEONS & DRAGONS is a collaborative game where you work with your friends to create your own stories. One person acts as a narrator, called a Dungeon Master, and the other players each take on the role of a hero, called a Player Character, in the adventuring party in a story. The Dungeon Master sets up a scene by describing a place and any threats that may exist, and then each player contributes ideas by explaining their own character's actions. With each scene created by the group, the story moves forward in unexpected and entertaining ways.

If you don't feel confident starting from scratch, you can go to your local gaming store and play a DUNGEONS & DRAGONS demonstration session. Demos can be a quick way to learn how the game is played and an opportunity to possibly make some brand-new friends at the same time.

After you've read through all the character options in this little magic manual, there's even more DUNGEONS & DRAGONS material out there to ignite your imagination. The *Monsters & Creatures* guide is bursting at the seams with beasts aplenty for you and your friends to defeat. *Warriors & Weapons* goes into more detail about the different adventuring races and the martial classes who can join you on your quest. The *Dungeons & Tombs* guide is filled with strange, sinister places for you and your friends to explore. You know who your hero is and have imbued them with magical might, now find out what dangers lurk in the darkness and *answer the call to adventure!*

Published in the United States by Ten Speed Press, an imprint of Random House, a division of Penguin Random House LLC, New York.
www.tenspeed.com

Ten Speed Press and the Ten Speed Press colophon are registered trademarks of Penguin Random House LLC.

Library of Congress Cataloging-in-Publication Data
Names: Zub, Jim author. | Conceptopolis, illustrator. | Ten Speed Press. |
    Wizards of the Coast, Inc.
Title: Wizards & spells : a young adventurer's guide. Dungeons & dragons /
    written by Jim Zub, with Stacy King and Andrew Wheeler ; [illustrations
    by Conceptopolis].
Other titles: Wizards and spells
Description: First Edition. | California : Ten Speed Press, [2019] |
    Audience: Grades: 4 to 6.
Identifiers: LCCN 2019019996 | ISBN 9781984856463 (Hardcover) |
    ISBN 9781984856470 (eBook)
Subjects: LCSH: Dungeons and dragons (Game)—Handbooks, manuals,
    etc—Juvenile literature. | Computer games—Juvenile literature. |
    Fantasy games—Juvenile literature. | Wizards—Juvenile literature. |
    Role playing. | Mathematics. | Shared virtual environments. | Fantasy
    tabletop role-playing game.
Classification: LCC GV1469.62.D84 Z839 2019 | DDC 793.93—dc23
LC record available at https://lccn.loc.gov/2019019996

Hardcover ISBN: 978-1-9848-5646-3
eBook ISBN: 978-1-9848-5647-0

Printed in China

Publisher: Aaron Wehner
Art Director and Designer: Betsy Stromberg
Editor: Julie Bennett
Managing Editor: Doug Ogan
Production Designer: Lisa Bieser
Production Manager: Dan Myers
Wizards of the Coast Team: David Gershman, Kate Irwin, Adam Lee, Hilary Ross, Liz Schuh
Illustrations: Conceptopolis, LLC

10 9 8 7 6 5 4 3 2

First Edition